The **50**
Best Games for
Groups

The 50 Best Group Games Pocket Books

The 50 Best Games for Building Self-Esteem
The 50 Best Games for Sensory Perception
The 50 Best Games for Brain Exercise
The 50 Best Games for Relaxation & Concentration
The 50 Best Games for Speech & Language Development
The 50 Best Games for Children's Groups
The 50 Best Games for Groups
The 50 Best Indoor Games for Groups

The **50** Best Games for **Groups**

Josef Griesbeck
translated by Lilo Seelos

HINTON**HOUSE**

Published by

Hinton House Publishers Ltd
Newman House, 4 High Street, Buckingham, MK18 1NT, UK

info@hintonpublishers.com
www.hintonpublishers.com

First published 2009
Reprinted 2011, 2013

Printed in the United Kingdom by Hobbs the Printers Ltd

British Library Cataloguing in Publication Data
Griesbeck, Josef.
  The 50 best games for groups. – (The 50 best group games pocket
  books ; 7)
  1. Group games
  I. Title II. Series III. Fifty best games for groups
  790.1'5-dc22

  ISBN-13: 9781906531164

Originally published in German by Don Bosco
Verlag München under the title *Die 50 besten
Gruppenspiele* © Don Bosco Verlag, München 2005

FSC
www.fsc.org
MIX
Paper from
responsible sources
FSC® C020438

Contents

Contents

'Playing is an activity that cannot
be taken seriously enough'

– *Jean Jacques Cousteau*

Four Corners

Ask everyone to spread out around the room. Then ask group members to choose one corner of the room according to a given topic such as, for example, 'How do you spend the majority of your time at the moment?':

- ☼ Those people who spend most of their time at school or at work, go to corner 1.

- ☼ Those people who have the most free time, go to corner 2.

- ☼ Those people who spend most of their time with their family, go to corner 3.

- ☼ Those people who spend most of their time with friends or with a partner, go to corner 4.

Once everyone has found their corner, groups can discuss with each other how they spend their time.

Variation for Children

- ☼ What is your favourite TV programme at the moment (choose from one of four)?

- ☼ Where would you like to live one day (city, country, abroad, at home)?

- ☼ Where do you most like to be (at home, in the country, in a town, at a swimming pool)?

Reporter Game

Tell the group that they are all to become investigative reporters. Give each person a task list. Group members then have to find people to match the descriptions on their list by asking each other questions and write their names next to each description.

Examples

A good dancer
Has climbed up the Eiffel Tower
Is a vegetarian
Is a football fan
Drives a big car
Is a Science Fiction fanatic
Likes to eat spinach
Has more than one brother or sister

Prognosis

This game is best played with everyone sitting in a circle. One player starts by making a statement and giving three possible responses.

For example: All pubs and restaurants should have smoking room!

1 I am all for it

2 I think that is out of the question

3 I don't care

The person who made the proposal now indicates their choice by putting their hand behind their back and holding up one, two or three fingers.

Everyone else now predicts what they think that player's choice is by showing either one, two or three fingers on their own hands. Then the proposer reveals their choice by revealing their hand.

☼ How many people were right?

☼ Why did they make that assumption?

My Name is ...

Start by holding up a flower and saying: 'My name is Anna and I say this is a flower'. Then they explain: 'I am now going to pass this flower around the circle to Carl. Then Carl has to say: "My name is Carl. Anna and Carl say that this is a flower".'

All members of the group take turns to continue in this way, with players having to repeat increasing numbers of names as the game progresses around the circle.

It will quickly become obvious that the last person in the group is going to have the hardest task. If a group consists of fewer than ten people, you could go around the circle twice to make the game more challenging for all players.

Make sure you help out anyone who gets stuck – remember that the group members won't have much experience of recalling names.

Variation

Pass a small bag is around the circle. Explain that the group is going to pack the bag to go on a trip. Players have to say their names and something they are going to pack in the bag, for example, a toothbrush, before passing on the bag to the next person. The next player then has to say their name and something else to add to the packing list, before listing everything in the bag, for example, 'I'm Stuart and I am adding socks. Now there is a toothbrush and some socks in the bag.'

The game continues this way around the circle until everybody has packed something into the bag.

Crossword Game

Place a large piece of paper in the middle of the floor. Depending on the age and number of players draw a number of lines or a basic crossword framework on the piece of paper, or the paper can be left blank for the crossword to grow by itself.

One player starts by writing their first name in the crossword puzzle, either horizontally or vertically. Then a second player adds their name, linking it with a letter of the name that has already been written down. Continue in this way until everyone in the group has had a turn.

Then players can add further information that they consider to be important about themselves. It is advisable to agree topics to focus on for this additional information, for example, city or road names, family names, favourite colours, and so on.

Guessing Names

Why some people's names can seem to be closely linked to their personalities is likely to remain a mystery. No doubt everyone has had an experience where the name of an unfamiliar person has conjured up some very specific images, which were actually confirmed on meeting the person. This can be put to the test if group members do not yet know each other.

Game 1

One player starts by sitting in the middle of the circle. All other players who do not yet know the person's name have a go at guessing it and write their guess on a piece of paper. This can be a fun exercise for everyone!

Game 2

All members of the group write their own first name on a piece of paper. Collect the pieces of paper, shuffle them and then hand them out again. Players then take it in turns to give the piece of paper with the unfamiliar name to the person they believe it belongs to.

Discussion

☼ How many names were guessed correctly, how many were not?

☼ What kind of (subconscious) reasons might have been behind the different guesses?

☼ Does anyone know any reason that may have played a role in their having been given their particular name?

Video Contact

This game is particularly suitable for groups where participants do not yet know each other or know each other only fleetingly. For example, after welcoming people who are arriving on their own at a conference, youth hostel, or in a seminar room, the leader could ask individual participants whether it would be OK to record a brief video clip of them. Hopefully no one will mind!

Once everyone has got together and been welcomed, the group leader can start the video game.

Examples

Clips are shot in such a way that initially only a participant's mouth can be seen. The video is paused briefly and participants try to work out who the mouth belongs to. Then the video continues, revealing all of the participant's face…

Or you could start just by showing people's hair or their feet walking across the room.

Eagle Eyes

A detective has to have good observational skills as well as being able to remember details. These skills can be practised within the group.

Ask everyone to close their eyes, and lower their heads, or cover their eyes with their hands to ensure no looking can take place! Now ask a question about the group, for example, 'Who is wearing a red jumper? Without opening your eyes, please, point to or in the direction of that person. Open your eyes!' Now everyone can look to see who is wearing a red jumper and whether they guessed correctly. Then the game continues along similar lines.

Variations

One group member leaves the room and two others change places. Then the player outside comes back into the room and has to guess who has changed places.

As above, but this time players swap an item of clothing.

Mystery People

Ask each person to write their name on a piece of paper, collect these in, shuffle them and then randomly hand them out again.

Now, each member of the group must come up with a personal description of the person whose name they have been given.

The description should be in the form of statements, starting with information that does not immediately reveal the person in question. The description should gradually become more precise, enabling the other group members to narrow down their guesses as to who it could be. In the end, the description can become really obvious so that everyone will be able to guess who the person is.

Players then take it in turn to read out their descriptions for everyone to guess.

Variation

The person reading out their description can divide it into three parts. When someone has guessed the mystery person's identity they should write the name on a piece of paper along with the number 1, 2 or 3 depending on when they guessed.

How many people guessed the identity at each stage?

The Guinness Book
of Records Game

Everyone has some kind of special skill or personal record they can tell to the group.

Invite each person in the group to name something that is associated with some kind of achievement, record or top performance. For example, if Sam claims to have the most aunts, she will have to specify how many aunts she has got. If there is someone else in the group who has got even more aunts, then that person will receive the Guinness Book of Records award.

All records and names should be written on a large piece of paper and posted in a prominent place on the wall.

Ideas for records:

I have got the most books.
I can do the most push-ups.
My class has got the highest number of pupils.

Happy Families Rhymes

Ask the group to stand in a circle. Start by giving the group the following explanation:

> 'I am going to give everyone a small card, which has got a surname written on it. In this game, every family consists of a father, a mother, a son, a daughter and a grandmother. So, for example, one of you may get a card that will have "Father Rice" written on it. When I give you a signal, you must all try to find your family members and get together in your family groups. You are allowed to call out the family name that is written on your card. Families who have found all their members must sit down together in a circle. The family that sits down first is the winner.'

There is one more important rule. As soon as you have been given a card you have to pass it on, face-down, around the circle. As the cards continue to pass around the circle, you will also receive cards, which again you have to pass on. Keep passing the cards around until I shout 'Go!'. This is the signal to look at your card and for families trying to find each other.'

Examples

Choose family names that rhyme to make the game harder – Rice, Mice, Dice, Nice, Slice, Spice, Price, and so on.

If you are playing with a group of children, names taken from popular children's books or TV programmes work particularly well.

Please note: there will be a lot of shouting. Make sure you play this game where it is not going to disturb anybody else.

Radio Contact

Players sit in a circle and take turns counting through the circle. Everybody has to remember their number.

Now start the game by raising both your arms and signalling numbers using your fingers. At the same time those on either side of you join in using the hand closest to you, in other words, the neighbour on your left uses their right hand, the neighbour on your right uses their left hand.

At the same time say: 'I am chief radio operator Number 1 and I am radioing chief radio operator Number 7 [for example].' Contact is made with player Number 7, who has to raise their hands and, obviously, their neighbours also have to join in. Then Number 7 starts all over again: 'I am chief radio operator Number 7 and I am radioing …'

If someone forgets to radio another player, forgets to join into their neighbour's radioing attempt or radios by mistake when it is not their turn, that player has to stand up. If a player makes a second mistake, they have to kneel down, and so on.

Variation 1

Each player chooses an animal name. For example, Rosie is an owl and calls out 'bull'. Whoever is 'bull' responds by making a mooing noise and then calls out 'cockerel'. The cockerel crows and calls out …

Variation 2

Each player chooses the name of a plant (or flower). Peter starts by saying, 'My pigeons are flying to "sweet corn".' Whoever is 'sweet corn' has to react immediately: 'My pigeons are flying to "potatoes".' And so on.

Clapping Round

All group members sit in a circle and take turns counting around the circle. At the same time, everyone should slap their hands on their thighs, then clap their hands together and finally click their fingers, first with their right hand, then with their left. Then they start this rhythm all over again.

This is where the interesting part begins: It is best if you start. When you click the fingers of your right hand like everyone else, you call out your own number; when you click the fingers of your left hand, randomly call out another player's number. Without halting the rhythm, the player whose number has been called out has to say their own number when they click the fingers of their right hand and a new random number when they click the fingers of their left hand.

Anyone who get it wrong, for example, by missing their turn or getting the rhythm wrong, have to pay a forfeit before restarting the game.

Variation 1

To make things a little easier, first names could be called out instead of numbers.

Variation 2

The rhythm could gradually be increased or, which is even more difficult, the number of claps could be reduced to three: slapping your thighs ('one'), clapping your hands together ('call out'), clicking the fingers of both hands at the same time ('say a random number').

Dibble-Dabble

Give each person in the group a number, starting at one.

The first person starts by saying, 'I am Dibble-Dabble number 1 with no dibble! Dibble-Dabble number 8, how many dibbles do you have?' Player number 8 now says the same thing, using their own number and stating the number of dibbles they have.

The game starts to become interesting when a player makes a mistake. Then that player is given a 'dibble' (a dot) on their forehead or in front of them on the floor (you could use chalk). That player now has to bear in mind that they have one 'dibble' when their number is called out again.

I Can't Believe It

Ask one of the group members to wait outside the room. The people left in the room come up with an animal that the person outside will have to mime, for example, a monkey.

Now ask the person outside to come back into the room and mime a monkey for those in the room to guess. While that person is acting out their mime, the other members of the group call out all sorts of animal names, but not 'monkey'. For example, if the person miming starts jumping about, they could call out 'kangaroo' or 'rabbit', even though the jumping is clearly being accompanied by 'monkey movements'.

Fragrant Chairs

The group leader claims that Lucy can use only her sense of smell in order to guess which of three chairs in the middle of the room has been selected by the rest of the group in Lucy's absence. Indeed, when Lucy returns to the room, she will sniff each chair and will know which was selected by the other group members.

This is how it works: The leader uses a specific system when calling Lucy back in. If the leader calls out, 'Come!' (one word), it is the first chair on the left that has been chosen. If the leader calls out, 'Come in!' it is the middle chair, and if the leader calls out, 'We are ready', it is the third.

Variation 1

The leader can use gesture to indicate the chair, for instance, placing both hands on their left thigh (left chair), crosses their arms (middle chair) or placing them on their right thigh (right chair).

Variation 2

Line up the chairs along the wall opposite the door. If the leader addresses the person as soon as they come in, it is the first chair; if he or she addresses them in the middle of the room, it is the middle chair and if they are only addressed when they have reached the chairs, it is the third chair.

Boss & Secretary

Four group members are chosen to be the bosses and are asked to stand in the four corners of the room. Each boss is now allowed to choose a secretary. However, these are then swapped diagonally across the room.

At a signal, each boss has to dictate a letter to their secretary, who is now standing in the corner opposite to them. As you can imagine play will be rather noisy and chaotic. Secretaries are not allowed to use any shorthand and must take down their letter in full. The winner is the person who finishes their letter first (the number of words should be agreed before the game starts and should be the same for everyone).

Instead of making up letters, articles of similar lengths could be cut out from newspapers and read out.

Doing the Opposite

One member of the group starts by calling someone's name and then saying, for example, 'eye' while pointing to their knee. The person whose name has been called out now has to do the opposite, i.e., point to their eye and say 'knee'. Then this person names someone else and says, for example, 'arm' while pointing to their toes.

18

Circle Games

A variety of quick and easy games can be played within the group.

☼ Place one pencil across two other pencils. One player has to pick up the two pencils underneath and lift and pass the top pencil on to the next player, who must use two pencils to receive that pencil and then pass it on to the next person.

☼ An empty matchbox is passed nose to nose between players without using hands.

☼ A coin is passed from the back or index finger of one player's hand to the back or index finger of another player's hand.

☼ A table tennis ball is passed around the circle using spoons or bats. Group members are not allowed to use their hands to touch the ball.

☼ A ruler is placed horizontally on one player's index finger and has to be passed around the circle from index finger to index finger.

☼ One player holds a drinking straw (or something similar) between nose and upper lip. Players have to try to pass the straw around the circle without using their hands.

☼ Players have to hold an orange between chin and neck and pass the orange around the circle without using their hands.

☼ Players have to roll a table tennis ball from a bat onto the top of an open bottle and then pass on the ball onto the next player's bat by tilting the bottle.

☼ All players hold a straw in their mouths. A ring is passed from straw to straw.

☼ Appropriately sized inflatable rings are placed over players' heads, so that they rest on the tips of the players' noses. Who can move the ring down to their neck first? No hands allowed!

☼ At a signal, blindfolded players start connecting 10 paperclips. The fastest player wins.

☼ Several players compete to wind up a piece of string whose end is attached to a bottle. This could be done across obstacles. The first person to wind up their piece of string and get their bottle is the winner.

☼ Ask players to move empty bottles from one room to another, without using their hands (for example, pushing the bottles with their feet).

☼ Ask players to blow a table tennis ball from one egg cup into a neighbouring egg cup.

☼ Ask players to pass a newspaper from one person to the next with their feet.

☼ Ask players to use a straw to suck up a piece of tissue paper and pass it on to the next player using straws only.

The Maze

Ask the members of the group to line up in several rows, one behind the other. The distance between the rows needs to be large enough for players to be able to stretch out their arms and not touch anything or anybody (see drawing A).

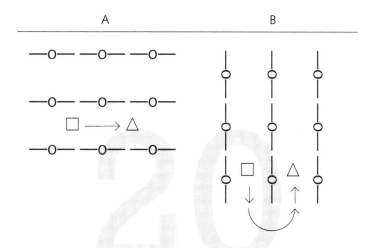

One player (the cat) now chases another player (the mouse) through the alleyways created by the group. The mouse is allowed to whistle (or clap) at any time. Then all players have to immediately turn 90 degrees (see drawing B), changing the direction of the alleyways from the previous direction. Neither cat nor mouse are allowed to slip through under anybody's arms.

Open Scissors

Players sit on chairs in a circle. The leader passes a pair of scissors to the person on their right and says: 'I am passing these open scissors', even though the scissors are actually closed. The next player now has to pass on the scissors and say whether they are passing open or closed scissors. Every time the scissors are passed on, the leader indicates whether that player has got it right.

The secret: Anybody who has their legs or even just their ankles crossed, has to say 'closed', all other players have to say 'open'. Players who manage to work out the solution should remain quiet and continue playing until the majority have worked out the solution or the leader calls a halt to the game.

Goat, Wolf & Cabbage

A shepherd wants to get across a river with his goat, because he thinks that the pasture is better on the other side. The shepherd also has a wolf and a basket full of cabbages, which are his only source of food. The shepherd has build a raft out of sticks, but the raft is too small to carry everything across the river in one go, he has to take one item at a time

The shepherd thinks:

☼ If I take the wolf across the river first, then the goat is bound to eat my cabbages.

☼ If I take the goat across first and then the wolf, the wolf is going to eat the goat while I fetch the cabbages.

What should the shepherd do?

First he takes the goat across to the other side. On his second crossing he takes the basket with the cabbages across, but brings the goat back again. Then he takes the wolf across and finally he comes back to collect the goat. (From an 8th Century abbey chronicle)

Can You Understand Me?

When people talk to each other it is really important that they express themselves in such a way that the person they are talking to understands what they mean. This is particularly important when someone explains the rules of a game to a group of players. The following exercise helps train the group members' ability to express themselves and to communicate effectively.

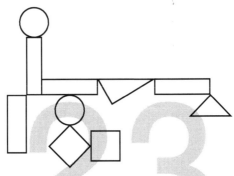

One player is given a piece of paper with a drawing on it. They must now describe the drawing for the others to copy without showing it to any of the other players. The others try to follow the instructions given without clarifying or checking back.

When the task is completed, the group then evaluate the results together:

☼ Did they get the order correct?

☼ Are the sizes right?

If ten symbols are linked to each other within one task, it will be easier for players work out their success quota using percentages.

These exercises can be repeated several times using different drawings. Players could also compare how they do when they are allowed to clarify and check back. It is likely that their success quota will increase significantly.

Don't Say 'Yes' or 'No'

Group members spread out around the room. At a signal, players pair up and start a conversation. While engaged in conversation, they are not allowed to say 'yes' or 'no'. If, during the conversation, someone says 'yes' or 'no', they lose their partner and have to find another when someone else become free.

The group will find that it does not take long to work out a questioning strategy to try to trick each other into saying 'yes' or 'no'.

You should draw the exercise to a close when it seems that most people have had a turn at speaking with each other.

Variation

One way to make the task easier is to ban players from saying 'yes', 'no', 'black' or 'white'. This way it is easier to trick another player by saying, for example, 'You just said "black"!' to which the other player may well respond with a 'No!'.

Wanted Poster

Divide the group into several smaller groups of 4 or 5 people.

Write a name on each of the poster-sized pieces of cardboard. Names should be those of well known and familiar people such as teachers, group leaders, and so on. Roll up the posters. Ask each group to select one of the rolls.

Group members now have to search the magazines and newspapers for suitable and funny pictures and pieces of text or headlines for their poster. These are cut out and stuck on the piece of cardboard. This way, group members create 'Wanted' posters for the person whose name is on the piece of cardboard.

Once complete, the posters can then be reviewed by the whole group afterwards.

Materials

Scissors, glue, old magazines and newspapers, and a poster-sized piece of cardboard for each group.

What, Why, Where, How

Ask each group member to think of something that they particularly like but not to tell anyone else. To help everyone understand how to use their idea, explain how the activity will work. People will be asked questions in a set order to reveal their like to the rest of the group.

It is Annette's turn first and let's say she has decided on ice cream. The person sitting to Annette's right now asks: 'Why do you love it?' Annette's answer might be: 'Because it is just so delicious.' The next person in the circle asks: 'Where do you love it?' She answers: 'Actually, anywhere.' Next question: 'How do you love it?' Possible answer: 'With strawberries.' The next question has to start with 'why' again:

☼ Why? – It just tastes so good.

☼ Where? – I quite like it in an Italian restaurant.

☼ How? – Eaten slowly, because it is so cold.

At about this time, it should be obvious to nearly everyone that Annette is talking about ice cream.

Then it is the next person's turn.

Merchant of Paris

The activity starts with someone collecting scarves, jackets and similar items of clothing brought in by the members of the group. Ideally they should be placed in a basket. Alternatively, food or flowers could be placed in the basket.

Then the person who has collected in all the items starts by saying:

'I am a merchant from Paris,
I have many a different thing.
I don't allow yes and don't allow no,
Nor allow crying or laughing.
Both red and white are forbidden too,
Which colour can I offer to you?'

Now the group members get involved in sales negotiations with the merchant, where no one is allowed to laugh, cry or say any of the words mentioned in the rhyme. If anyone slips up, they don't get their goods. Prior to starting the game, the group could also agree additional rules, for example, players who make a mistake have to take over from the merchant or pay a forfeit.

ABC Answers

The game starts with the leader or one of the members of the group asking a question, for example, 'Is this water drinkable?'

Everyone in the group then takes it in turns to think of one-word answers to the question. The initial letters of the answers must follow the order of the letters of the alphabet, for example, 'absolutely', 'barely', 'completely', 'doubtful', 'earthy', 'fabulous', 'grim', etc.

To make this activity more difficult, ask people to think of two-word answers, where both words have to start with the same letter: 'absolutely alluring', 'brilliantly bottled', 'dirty dishwater', 'earthy extract', 'fabulously fizzy', 'ghastly garbage', and so on.

Paying a Forfeit

Many of the games in this book can be combined with paying forfeits. For example, if a player gets a mark, a minus point or has lost a round, they have to pay a forfeit. This should be something that is fun for everyone and should not involve any humiliating or personal tasks. It helps if you allow players to reject a proposed forfeit and request a different one.

Forfeit suggestions

☀ Whisper something nice in another person's ear.

☀ Give a small speech in praise of yourself.

☀ Give a small presentation about not smoking.

☀ Tell everyone about your best experience.

☀ Tell everyone a story from your childhood.

☀ Try to touch your toes without bending your knees.

☀ Make up a sentence that does not contain the letter 'r'.

☀ Choose a mealtime-related chore.

☀ Sing a newspaper headline to a tune chosen by the group.

☀ Sit on the floor and then stand up without using your hands.

☀ List five things you would do if you won the lottery.

☀ Have your face painted with a moustache.

☀ Laugh for 30 seconds.

☀ Whistle (not blow!) out a candle.

☀ Wear a blindfold and find an object that has been dropped audibly.

☀ Write a poem or a short story.

The Truth Game

The language we use, and the way we speak, gives away a lot about ourselves.

Sometimes we might suspect that what is being said does not correspond to reality. In this activity group members can see how good they are at spotting when people are not telling the truth.

Ask everyone to think of an event that has happened to them in their lives. Now each person takes it in turns to tell the group their story, but they must include something that isn't true.

Once the story has ended see how many people were bale to spot the made up section.

Group Theatre

Everyone in the group can get involved to make this a great spectacle. Begin by explaining that: 'A famous singer is going to perform here soon, so we need to make the necessary preparations. First of all, we need a curtain. Who wants to be the curtain?'

The curtain volunteer must mime turning a handle by the side of the stage and make a squeaking sound to indicate the movement of the curtains being pulled up. After a quick 'curtain rehearsal', the preparations continue: 'Ladies and Gentlemen, this is going to be an open-air performance in the woods, so we need some trees. Who would like to be tree?'

Several participants can volunteer for this and briefly rehearse swaying to and fro in the wind. 'Now we need someone to be responsible for the wind.' Wind volunteers should stand on one side of the stage and briefly rehearse blowing as hard as they can. 'Now we need a moon.' The person who is playing the moon can rehearse moving slowly onto the stage from the side and climbing up on a chair.

It is likely that there will still be some members of the group sitting down. 'And finally, we will need some rain. Please, everyone who is sitting down, can you tap your fingers on the table.'

Now say: 'In order to make sure everything will be alright for the actual performance, we need to do a dress rehearsal. The curtain opens and the moon slowly comes up. The wind blows and it starts raining. The trees sway backwards and forwards on this rainy night. And then, the artist appears...'

Now you should climb on to a chair and announce: 'Ladies and Gentlemen! I am afraid our artist has caught a cold in this awful weather. Unfortunately we will have to cancel tonight's performance!'

The Fantasy Game

Discover the secret thoughts of everyone present while having great fun playing the game!

Preparation: Make a list of silly questions and have pens and pencils readily available. Read out the questions and give the group two minutes to write down their best, original answer.

Examples

What would you do if your bed was attached to a hot air balloon?

☼ … if you were Emperor of Greenland?

☼ … if having a beard was the law?

☼ … if you had not been born?

Afterwards, you could simply read out answers for fun or you could combine this with a guessing game. For instance, collect in all pieces of paper and select a few answers to read aloud.

After reading out an answer, everyone can have a guess as to who may have written it.

Who am I?

Ask one person to leave the room. The remaining group members agree on an object, for example, a mirror. Then the person outside is called back in and has to guess the object by asking questions. The questions can only be answered using 'Yes' or 'No'.

To make the game competitive, you could keep track of the number of 'No's' to identify who has been quickest to guess the object.

Variation 1

Choose a famous person instead of an object. The person guessing could start by trying to find their profession - 'Is it an actor?'

For fun, you could choose the guesser themselves.

Variation 2

Ask the group to get together in pairs and find out each other's favourite meal by asking 'Yes'/'No' questions.

Zoo Game

This game is suitable for 8 to 20 players. Everyone playing must choose an animal name, which they will keep throughout the game. They should keep their name a secret.

One person starts by saying, 'I was at the zoo and saw a lot of animals, but the zebra seemed to be missing.' This is based on the assumption that one of the players has chosen to be a zebra.

The person who has chosen to be a zebra responds by saying, 'The zebra was there, but the giraffe [for example] was missing.' The person who has chosen to be a giraffe then has a turn. If the chosen animal isn't present, or if anyone spends too long thinking an animal, a forfeit can be performed.

☼ Does anyone get to the end of the game without having a forfeit?

☼ Is there anyone left whose animal has not been guessed?

Dancing Games

The following are brief outlines of the best dancing games. These can be developed further and adapted according to your group or gathering. Most require minimal props – usually only chairs, pens and paper and a basket or other container.

Divide your group into boys/men and girls/women. Each boy is given half a paper heart. The other halves of the hearts are given to the girls. Similarly, the dancers could be given one half of a symbol or a quotation. Now the search can begin. Couples who have found each other can start dancing.

Write occupations or actions on pieces of paper, ensuring there are two of each. Give one piece to the boys and one to the girls. At a signal, everyone must start to mime their occupation or action without making a sound. Dance partners have to recognise each other by finding the person performing the same actions.

Variations

Animal sounds. At a signal, dancers start making animal noises and pair up by listening out for someone making the same animal sound. This game is also fun when played in the dark.

When the music stops, everyone has to sit down. The last person to sit down is out. Once several people are out, they can provide or accompany the music by singing!

Stop the music and call out a number. Dancing couples have to get together in groups to make up that number, for example, '6' is three couples, '3' is one couple plus one person from another pair. Anyone left over is out.

Gentlemen are given cards with numbers 1 to … depending on the number of men. The same for the ladies. Those with the same numbers dance with each other. For the next song all ladies (or gentlemen) place their number in a basket and draw out new numbers. Instead of numbers you could use pairs of identical post cards or autumn leaves.

Basket dance. Three chairs are lined up in a row. One lady sits in the middle with a gentleman sitting on each side. The lady is given a basket full of sweets. When the music starts, the lady offers the basket to one of the gentlemen, who takes a sweet which makes up for the lady then starting to dance with the other man. The gentleman with the basket then sits on the middle chair and quickly two ladies sit down at his sides. The game continues until everyone is dancing. It is really important that the empty places on the right or left of a dance partner are filled up quickly.

All ladies place an item from their handbag into a basket or box. Then the gentlemen are allowed to choose one item each. Now they must look for the owner of that item and, once they have found them, start dancing. This activity can be repeated by placing all items back in the basket/box and choosing again. All the gentlemen remove a shoe and place it in the middle of the room without the ladies looking, the ladies must the select a shoe and look for its owner.

Snowball waltz. One couple starts dancing. After about 20 seconds the lady chooses a new gentleman to dance with, and her original partner chooses a new lady. Now there are two couples dancing. The same process is repeated after a further 20 seconds, and so on, until everyone is moving about on the dance floor.

Each pair of dancers must keep an orange or a balloon between their foreheads while they are dancing. They cannot use their hands to correct the position of the orange/balloon. Any couple who drops their orange/balloon is out. The group should decide beforehand whether it will be acceptable for the orange/balloon to slide down to eye level. A number of observers will be needed whose task it is to ensure that the dancers keep moving.

Gentlemen hold balloons in their left hand, the ladies a pin. The men have to try to protect their balloons while the ladies try to burst other couples' balloons. Any couple that loses their balloon is out. Those who are out can form a circle around the couples still dancing. With this game, the balloon popping tends to dominate the activity rather than the dance. Nevertheless everyone should try to keep dancing.

Couples dance through an alley made from bottles. Any couple that knocks over a bottle is out!

Each couple is given a large sheet of newspaper, which has been folded as small as possible. Every time the music stops, dancers have to unfold their newspaper as quickly as possible and stand with their partner on their sheet. The last couple to stand on their sheet of newspaper is out. Sheets of newspaper must be quickly folded up again before the game can restart.

Dancers are paired up by having the same month of birth, same hair colour and so on. It is particularly important during this game to focus on having fun and not be too rigid about who dances with whom. Look out for those trying to cheat to be with their partner!

Couples Musical Chairs. Line up as many chairs back to back as there are couples. Remove one chair while the music is playing. The couples have to dance around the chairs. When the music stops, each couple has to try to get a chair and sit on it. The couple that has not got a chair is out. Another chair is taken away and the game continues.

Dancers have to find a new partner when they hear a previously agreed signal (blowing a trumpet, whistle sound, etc) or when the music stops.

The gentlemen (or the ladies) note down some items of information that have been agreed by the group beforehand (for example, occupation, number of pets). Pieces of paper are collected in and then given out to the other sex. Then the search and subsequent dancing can begin. Monitor the information to make sure that the information will not be offensive to other group members.

One person walks around on their own carrying a broom stick while everyone else is dancing. When they loudly drop the broom stick, everyone has to change partners. Anyone left without a partner picks up the broom stick, and the game continues.

A hat is passed from couple to couple or placed on the head of one dancer at a time. The couple who is in possession of the hat when the music stops is out.

Lantern dance. This game is particularly useful when there are several people without a dance partner; it is also great for bringing a dance to a close. Each person without a partner is given a lantern and all other lights are switched off. They hand the lantern to someone else and can then dance with that person's partner. The person who has received the lantern then has to find themselves a new dance partner by passing the lantern on to someone else.

Excuse-me dance. Anyone who has not found a dance partner walks up to a dancing couple, claps their hands and 'kidnaps' the lady or gentlemen. The dance partner who has been 'robbed' now has to find themselves a new dance partner by walking up to another dancing couple and clapping their hands, and so on.

I Bet I Can ...

Any member of the group can walk up to another person and propose a bet. The person who has been addressed can accept the bet or reject it.

If an agreement is reached between the two, the bet stands. This game could be organised so that two people at a time carry out the bet while everyone else is watching. However, it is also possible for everyone to play at the same time. Here are some examples for possible bets:

☼ I bet I know who you went to the cinema with last week!

☼ I bet I have more aunts than you.

☼ I bet that I have fewer fillings than you.

☼ I bet I can recite the twelve-times table more quickly than you.

Things in Common

You will need paper and pens for this activity.

Friendships or relationships stand the greatest chance of long-term success when partners have a number of interests in common. While this is not a guarantee for a successful long-term relationship, it at least provides a good foundation. This game is all about finding things in common and the whole group is invited to join into the search for these.

To start with, ask everyone to write their name on the top of a strip of paper followed by something they like or dislike. Encourage people to complete as many strips of paper as possible. Ideally, they should complete at least ten strips of paper.

Examples of likes or dislikes could include shopping, knitting, mountaineering, listening to classical music, playing or watching sport, and so on.

Now start exchanging strips of paper among the group. People are allowed to keep someone else's strip of paper if they find that person has written the same thing as them. The aim is to collect as many strips of paper from the others as possible.

☼ Discuss the group's likes and dislikes.

☼ Have people found things in common with others that they had not previously known about?

☼ Did anyone have a like that no one else shared?

Raffle of Favours

You will need paper and pens for this activity. It is a good way to end a course or a group session.

This is a raffle with favours and help as prizes, rather than physical objects. Invite anyone who would like to offer a 'prize' to write it on a piece of paper, followed by their name. People can offer more than one prize if they like.

In order for this to be a proper raffle, there should be twice or three times as many raffle tickets as there are people in the group.

Examples of prizes

☀ I will give you a photo or picture of your choice.

☀ I will go for a walk with you.

☀ I will take you out to the cinema.

☀ I'll invite you for a coffee at your favourite café.

☀ I will write you a short story.

☀ I will paint you a picture.

☀ I will help you in the garden.

☀ I will take you ice skating one evening.

☀ I will take your dog for a walk.

All pieces of paper should be folded up and placed into a container. The group will then need to agree how many raffle tickets are going to be drawn, just a few, or one for each person?

Follow My Voice!

The basis of this game is very simple. The group splits into pairs, one person says something and their partner listens to it. However, there is rather more to it than that ...

Players get together in pairs and stand opposite each other. One person in each pair has their eyes closed or is blindfolded. Their partner takes on the role of leader. They must repeat a story or something that has happened recently while walking backwards around the room watching their blindfolded partner. The blind person has to follow their partner but can only orientate by listening to their partner speak. Because there are other couples on the move at the same time, the game can become quite taxing.

Afterwards partners swap roles and, finally, everyone gets together to talk about their experiences.

School of Yodelling

Divide the group into three for this game of yodelling in rounds.

A handsome boy met a beautiful girl and promised to take her dancing that evening. He sang:

> 'I will pick up you.' (Group one repeats this line in a yodelling manner.)

The neighbour's daughter heard about this and wanted to go too. So, the boy sang to her as well: 'I will pick up you too'. (Group two starts to sing.)

Word gets around quickly and all the girls from the village want to come, too. So, the boy finally sang: 'I will pick up all of you.' (Now it is group three's turn.)

And now sing rounds for as long as possible …

Chain of Events

This game is about observing others and tuning into what they are doing. It requires a little preparation by the group leader but the rules are simple. The group members must work together to act out a scenario.

Each person is given a piece of paper outlining their specific role. They are given no other information. In other words, no one knows what kind of role the other players have been given, nor what the overall scenario is.

This means that most members of the group will first have to work out what the game is all about and who the key people are. Some people may already have more of an idea than others, but can only become active when everyone has carried out the task assigned to them.

All this should take place without talking!

Afterwards, you should make time for a discussion about how it went. Interesting points to discuss might be:

- ☼ How did people deal with and get over their own insecurities?

- ☼ How much did they have to tune into what others were doing?

- ☼ How did people respond to those who just acted out their part in the scenario without paying attention to anyone else?

- ☼ How did people respond to those who did not fulfil the task they were set?

Example

Someone is having their photo taken. Each participant is assigned one of the tasks below.

☼ Accompany someone who is going to have their photo taken.

☼ Your task is to take a photo of someone.

☼ You are responsible for sorting out the lighting for a photo shoot.

☼ A person is being photographed. You are responsible for sorting out a suitable background.

☼ You want to have your photo taken!

☼ You are a hair dresser, style someone's hair for a photo.

☼ You are a Golden Retriever and today you are going to have your photo taken with your owner.

☼ Someone is being photographed. You are the assistant to the photographer.

Repeat that Mime!

This is a fun game where players use mime to pass on information.

Ask between three and five people to go outside. One of the players who has remained in the room acts out a scenario, for example, 'being at the dentist' to the others. Encourage the 'actors' to make their mime as original and typical as possible and to exaggerate their mimed actions as much as they can.

One of the people outside is called in and another player now acts out the scenario for them. They must watch very carefully, because they will have to act out the same scenario for the next person to be called back in. The second person then mimes for the third person, and so on.

It is often quite amazing to see what, if anything, is left over from the original scenario by the end.

Who's on the Phone?

Divide the group into pairs and ask the partners to prepare to act out a 'telephone call'. They will each have to choose to be a well-known character or celebrity, but not tell their partner.

Once everyone has finished their preparations, the 'phone calls' can start. The first pair starts by 'ringing' each other, pretending to be their character, but not actually giving their names.

The aim of the game is to try to make it difficult for your partner to guess your identity.

Variation 1

Each person in a pair selects an identity for themselves. Then players ask each other 'Yes'/'No' questions to discover each others' identities.

Variation 2

The group leader tells Player A the identity of Player B and vice versa. They now know who their partner is, but don't know their own identity, which they must discover by asking questions about themselves.

Stage Potpourri

Potpourri means a medley of all kinds of things. This definition is the basis for the following game, which challenges group members to perform a scenario in a multitude of ways. For example:

☼ Player 1: 'I have lost my button!'

☼ Player 2: 'Yes, your highness, I will help you look for it!'

This scenario could be acted out in many different ways: as a play, an opera, an operetta, a detective story, a comedy, a tragedy, a Western, in a surreal manner, as a soap opera, and so on. Alternatively, the scene could be acted out without words, the actors could pretend to be drunk or assume characters, such as politicians, etc.

Shadow Games

To start with, people often have inhibitions about participating in this kind of game – until they get the bug!

Erect a 'shadow screen' for the group to use. This can be made easily by stretching a sheet (or several sheets sewn together) from one wall to another or between two trees. Position a spot light approximately four metres behind the screen, with the beam directed onto the screen.

Now demonstrate some shadow play for the group and then ask for volunteers to experiment and play about between the screen and the spotlight, as close as possible to the screen. This will help to facilitate creative acting.

Then give two players some actions to perform for the rest of the group.

Suggestions for shadow play

Simple hand movements, birds flying, wild animals and so on.

- ☼ Have several people work together to experiment with different hand movements.

- ☼ Two players could have a pretend boxing match. To do this, one person stands half a metre closer to the light than the other so that none of the boxers' punches actually hit anyone. This distance is not visible to the audience.

- ☼ Stick fighting. Two people each take hold of the ends of a stick. Then they can (gently) knock the centres of their sticks together, changing their stances regularly.

☼ Short fairytale scenarios, acted-out jokes, animal mimes, celebrities, and so on. Players may need some preparation time for this.

☼ Distinct routines such as a lecturing professor, a parade, a Japanese tea ceremony, putting on make up, ballet dancing and so on.

Note

Players should always try to stand sideways to show their profiles, facing either the screen or light will not work as well.

Any costumes used do not need to be very detailed, broad shapes work much better. Characters can be hinted at, through using, for example, an unusual hat, a long coat, an umbrella and so on.

Riding Waves

This game of trust requires a minimum of thirteen players.

The group lie down on the floor in a 'zig-zag pattern': in diagonal pairs head to head with one person stretching their legs to the right, the other to the left and touching the feet of the next pair, keeping close together. Now all players reach up their arms, palms facing upwards, to create a 'bed' or wave track.

One player stiffens their whole body and lies back (ideally helped by two others) onto the start of the wave track. It is important that they keep their body really stiff and their hands close to their body. The people making up the wave track then start using their hands to transport the person to the other end, where two people help them get off the track again. Players take turns to be carried by the wave.

As with all games of trust, participation should be voluntary and the group needs to get on well.

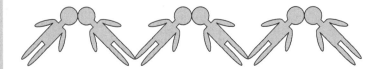

Let's Do Something Completely Different!

Many attempts have been made to discover what people look for in a holiday. One thing that comes time and again is people's desire to do something totally different ... This game attempts to do exactly that!

Each person must think about and discuss what they would like to do differently, this should be an enjoyable experience and not cause any ill feelings or trouble.

Here are some suggestions:

☼ To give a totally different present, for example, a pebble.

☼ Inviting complete strangers for breakfast.

☼ To serenade someone for their birthday.

☼ To walk around in pyjamas all day.

☼ To wear a mask while walking through a busy street.

☼ Boys/men wearing make up; women/girls wearing suits and ties.

Swaying Circle

In all groups and communities there are moments that are suitable for an activity that increases trust and solidarity. A swaying circle can be just thing for such a time.

Everyone in the group stands in a circle with their arms hanging down by their sides and their upper arms slightly touching their neighbour, reinforcing the idea of a strong bond between the group and that everyone is a link in a chain.

The leader also stands in the circle and directs the group: 'Everyone, close your eyes and take a few deep breaths. With our eyes closed we are going to try to create a swaying circle, where everyone moves gently from side to side as one.'

The leader can open their eyes from time to time and ask people to gently open their eyes when the swaying circle is in full motion. This way, people can not only feel, but see, the group swaying together as one.

Discussion

☼ Discuss how people experienced this exercise and how it made them feel.

☼ What did being part of such a group feel like?

☼ Where within the circle was there a feeling of great empathy and working together and where was this lacking?

☼ How did people feel when they were not working together?

Fox or Bear?

A person can be described as being 'as clever as a fox', 'as strong as an ox', 'as cuddly as bear' or 'as fast as a gazelle'.

These sorts of comparisons are often used to describe how we see and evaluate individual people. This game is all about making such comparisons.

Ask each person in the group to think of three animals that they would liken themselves to. It is important that they think carefully and are able to explain why they have chosen their particular animals.

Once everyone has decided on their animals, divide the group into pairs or small groups. Taking turns, each person chooses someone to liken to an animal. That person can respond by giving their view on the selection and whether it matches one of their own choices.

Discuss the range of animals within each group.

Variations

☼ Ask everyone to thinks about what kind of tree they might be. Before someone names their selection and explains why they have chosen it, others in the group can make their own suggestions for that person.

☼ Each person in the group writes down what musical instrument they would be. Collect the pieces of paper and shuffle them. Now players takes turns to select a piece of paper and read it out loud. The rest of the group must try to guess who has might have likened themselves to that instrument.

Whose is the Voice?

We tend to be able to recognise a familiar voice even at a distance, or when it is distorted or croaky. Even when members of the group have not known each other for very long, most of them will have already consciously or subconsciously learned to recognise other people's voices.

Divide everyone into two sub-groups, who stand opposite each other. Group A then all turn around so their backs are to the members of Group B.

The members of Group B quietly agree on a sound, perhaps an animal noise, and then choose one of their members to make that sound. Group A have to guess who it is.

Take turns for each person in the group to make a sound, and then swap over.

☼ Was one group better than the other at guessing?

☼ Was anyone's voice particularly easy to recognise?

☼ Was anyone's voice particularly difficult?